mainstreaming the visually impaired child:

blind and partially sighted students in the regular classroom

by
michael d. orlansky
university of virginia

thomas n. fairchild
series editor

danial b. fairchild
thomas n. fairchild
illustrators

Teaching Resources Corporation
100 Boylston Street, Boston, Massachusetts 02116, 617-357-8446

98475

Library of Congress Cataloging in Publication Data

Orlansky, Michael D
  Mainstreaming the visually impaired child

  (Mainstreaming series)
  1. Blind—Education.   2. Public schools.   I. Title.
HV1626.075   371.9'11   77-2152
ISBN 0-89384-016-5

Teaching Resources Corporation
100 Boylston Street, Boston, Massachusetts 02116
617-357-8446 · A New York Times Company

To Jan and Tamar, and to my parents, with love

To the children at Camp Wapanaki, Perkins, and the Washington State School for the Blind, who inspired the ideas contained in this book.

acknowledgments

I express my sincere appreciation to Mr. Lee W. Robinson, Deputy Superintendent, Idaho State School for the Deaf and the Blind, Gooding, Idaho, and to Miss Eileen Scott, Social Services Supervisor, Canadian National Institute for the Blind, Vancouver, British Columbia, for their careful reading of the manuscript, and for many helpful suggestions which were incorporated into the text.

Sister Margaret, Principal and first grade teacher, St. Mary's Elementary School, Moscow, Idaho, for reading the manuscript and providing a teacher's point of view.

Carolyn Fairchild, and Shellie West for cartoon ideas.

Marcy Taylor, Shellie West, and Ms. Lee Brydon for their assistance in the typing of the manuscript.

preface

In the past, educational needs of exceptional children were met by removing them from the "mainstream" of the regular classrooms, and serving them in a variety of segregated self-contained special classes. The trend in the '70's is educating exceptional children in the least restrictive educational setting; that is, as close as possible to their normal peers. This concept of "mainstreaming" exceptional children has received considerable support from within and outside the educational community. Although self-contained special classes will always be a meaningful alternative for some children, the personal and educational needs of many exceptional children can better be served in the regular class program with the supportive services of ancillary personnel and/or resource room help.

With the emphasis on "mainstreaming," the regular class teacher is now expected to meet the needs of exceptional children in his or her classroom along with all the other children in the class. The problem is that most regular class teachers have little or no preparation in the area of educating exceptional children. Regular class teachers need basic information regarding the various exceptionalities, and more specifically, practical suggestions which they can employ to enhance the "mainstreamed" exceptional child's personal and educational development.

The MAINSTREAMING SERIES was written to fill this need. Each book in the SERIES addresses itself to one area of exceptionality allowing teachers to select from the SERIES according to their interest or need. Each text provides information designed to eliminate misconceptions and stereotypes, and to improve the teacher's understanding of the exceptional child's uniqueness. Numerous practical suggestions are offered which will help the teacher work more effectively with the exceptional child in the "mainstream" of the regular classroom.

Currently, there is a great deal of controversy surrounding the use of categories and labels. The books in the SERIES are organized according to categories of exceptionality because the content within each book is only relevant for a child with a specific handicapping condition. The intent is not to propagate labeling; in fact, labeling children is inconsistent with the philosophy of the SERIES. The books address themselves to behaviors and how teachers can work with these behaviors in exceptional children. The books in the SERIES are categorized—not the children. The books are categorized in order to cue teachers to the particular content for which they might be looking.

There is much truth in the old saying, "A picture is worth a thousand words." A cartoon format was used for each book in the MAINSTREAMING SERIES as a means of sustaining interest and emphasizing important concepts. The cartoon format also allows for easy, relaxed reading. We felt that teachers, being on the firing line all day, would be more likely to read and refer to our material, than to a lengthy text filled with theory and jargon. Typical to cartooning is the need to exaggerate, stereotype, and focus on our weaknesses. I sincerely hope the cartoons do not offend any children, parents, or professionals, because that is not the purpose for which they were intended. They are intended to make you think.

I hope you find this book helpful in your work with mainstreamed exceptional children, or with any other children, since they are all special.

THOMAS N. FAIRCHILD
SERIES EDITOR

introduction

What is the visually impaired child like? Can children with little or no vision successfully join their sighted friends in regular classrooms? What can we, as teachers, do to help them in this process?

This book is designed to answer some of these questions, and to assist the teacher of blind and partially sighted children in the regular classroom.

Until recently, most visually impaired children were educated in residential schools for the blind. These schools continue to meet the needs of many visually impaired children today.

Educators of the visually impaired now generally agree, however, that it is beneficial in many ways for the child to live at home and attend a local school with sighted children. The visually impaired child can and should be a true member of his/her family and community. Your integrated classroom can do much to make this possible.

Teachers, principals, parents, and students are often apprehensive about having a visually impaired child join the regular class. This is understandable, since many of us have never known or worked with such a child. But teachers usually find that having a visually impaired child does not create major problems in the classroom. Only a few changes or adaptations are likely to be necessary. Most visually impaired children do not impose excessive demands upon the teacher's time.

The ideas and suggestions in this book are offered with the visually impaired child in mind, but many of them can apply to all students as well. A large part of effective teaching is "common sense."

The author hopes this book makes your experience with a visually impaired child a very positive one for both you and the child.

MICHAEL D. ORLANSKY

contents

chapter 1

**types of
visual
impairments**

Let's take a brief look at the types of visual impairments children in your class may have. While this is a general discussion of visual impairment, it is also important for the teacher to know the specific cause of the child's visual problem. Different eye conditions may require different strategies in the classroom. The teacher should know the amount and kind of the child's remaining vision, if any.

Basically, a child's vision can be impaired in 3 ways:

1. *Visual Acuity* may be reduced. The child may not see sharply or clearly, or may have to get very close to objects. Some children are unable to see fine details at any distance.

3

2. The *Field of Vision* may be restricted. While a normal eye takes in a wide area, an eye with limited field of vision may be able to see only a very small part of "the whole picture."

4

3. *Color Vision* may be defective. The child may not be able to distinguish certain colors.

5

Some children, of course, are totally blind. Naturally, their needs are different from those of children with impaired, but still useful, vision.

Some have *light perception only*, which would be similar to walking around with your eyes closed. You would be able to tell the difference between light and dark, but little else. However, light perception can be very helpful in traveling and other skills, if used effectively.

In this book, we will speak of the "visually impaired" child most of the time. We will use the "educational definitions" for blindness and partial sight:

The *Blind* child does not have enough vision to learn to read print, and needs instruction in reading braille.

The *Partially Sighted* child has enough vision to read print. Certain materials and modifications are necessary because of this child's limited vision.

With totally blind children, it is especially important for the teacher to know the age at which the child became blind.

A child who was born blind, or who became blind very early in life, will probably have a different picture of the world from a person who loses sight later in life.

A child who becomes blind after about 5 years of age usually keeps some kind of "visual memory." This can be very useful in education and adjustment.

We often speak of a person's having "20/20 vision." This is simply a convenient way of describing normal vision.

A child with 20/20 vision can see from a distance of 20 feet what a normal eye *should* be able to see at a distance of 20 feet.

A child with 20/400 vision can see from a distance of 20 feet what a normal eye should see at a distance of *400* feet. In other words, the object must be brought much closer for this child to see it clearly.

Such measurements can be helpful, but numbers do not tell us the whole story. Problems in field of vision, color vision, and light sensitivity can often go undetected in school.

It's most important to notice how a child *uses* his/her vision.

Some children have only a tiny amount of vision, and are very skillful at using it.

Other children have relatively good visual acuity, but are not able to use it very well. They may need practice in using their remaining vision.

chapter 2

how the
regular classroom
teacher can help

ENTERING THE REGULAR CLASS PROGRAM

Is our visually impaired child really ready to go to the local school? Pauline Moor (1952) suggests that for successful integration to take place, the child should at least be able to:

* 1.   Move about easily, with a fair sense of direction.

* 2.   Orient himself or herself to new people and places without too much difficulty.

* 3.   Leave home without becoming unduly upset.

*4. Make known his or her toilet needs.

*5. Take new experiences in stride, and show a certain amount of flexibility or adaptability.

*6. Express himself or herself reasonably clearly.

7. Feel comfortable about going to school, and look forward to it most of the time.

If the visually impaired child does not meet most of these standards, he or she may not be quite ready to join a regular class. The child may need additional help in certain areas, or perhaps just some extra time to develop.

Many studies have shown that the visually handicapped child does not differ from the normal child in intelligence; nor is there any correlation between intelligence and the age of the child at onset of blindness.

Of course, some children have other physical, mental, or behavioral problems in addition to a visual loss. A combination of serious disabilities can make education in the regular classroom difficult.

Visually impaired children are not really so "different."

Basically they have the same needs as other children. This is why we believe they should spend the maximum amount of time possible in the regular classroom.

ATTITUDES

Like all children, the visually impaired will respond to the way in which they are treated. In school, the teacher's attitude towards the child who is "different" sets an example for the rest of the class to follow.

... and this is where you will be seated.

Here are a few general "do's" and "dont's" for you to consider:

- •**Do** treat the visually impaired child naturally, as you would any other child.

- •**Do** plan activities *with* the visually impaired child, not *for* him/her.

- •**Do** allow the child to have some free, unstructured time to use as he/she likes, as you would for other children.

- •**Do** expect the child to meet reasonable standards of performance and behavior, as you would for the rest of the class.

- **Don't** avoid using such words as *see, look,* and *blind* in the child's presence. The visually impaired child will feel comfortable with them, and will probably use these terms naturally in conversation.

- **Don't** fuss over his/her accomplishments as "remarkable" or "wonderful" . . . visual impairment implies neither subnormality nor special gifts.

- **Don't** pity the child or feel you must make special arrangements for everything.

- **Don't** tolerate unacceptable behavior just because the child has a visual loss.

- **Don't** feel that *all* his/her difficulties and needs are due to the visual loss.

SOCIAL GROWTH

Your integrated classroom presents daily opportunities for the social growth and development of the student. Classmates generally accept visually impaired children in a natural way, although some may need extra encouragement. The effective teacher seeks to facilitate independence and cooperation among all students.

You will find that you need not always be "on top of" the visually impaired child.

THE DARING YOUNG MAN ON THE FLYING TRAPEZE...

At first, classmates may help a blind child move around
the classroom and building; later, the child should be
encouraged to travel independently wherever possible.

Friendly interaction with sighted children inside and out of the classroom can help the visually impaired child overcome social isolation. He/she can and should participate in extracurricular activities such as field trips, clubs, dances, picnics, sports, games, plays, and concerts.

Sometimes the child will need assistance, but you may also find that the visually impaired child is able to help sighted children in certain areas. By valuing his/her contributions, you can enhance the visually impaired child's feelings of independence and self-confidence.

We can help the visually impaired child develop socially acceptable behaviors. For example, encourage the child to face in the direction of the person with whom he/she is speaking. Don't be afraid to offer a polite reminder if the child is looking away from you, or mumbling unclearly.

Some visually impaired children may exhibit mannerisms; i.e., repetitive behaviors that can seem peculiar or even disturbing to teachers and classmates. These may include: rocking back and forth, eye poking, head rolling, hand waving, or gazing at bright lights. Different theories seek to explain such mannerisms. In most cases, these habits seem to grow out of a need for self-stimulation. The best approach is probably to keep the child involved in varied, interesting activities - especially activities using the hands. The child should not be punished or embarrassed in front of classmates if mannerisms occur, but may be quietly reminded of them.

MOBILITY

A teacher once told a story of a blind child who had great ability as a pianist. The child could play all of Beethoven's piano sonatas from memory - but he could never find his way to the piano, and had to be helped to and from it whenever he played.

Another blind child knew many facts about the history and geography of ancient Greece - but wasn't able to travel from her home to the store around the corner.

Such stories point out the extreme importance of *mobility* training for the severely visually impaired. Academics alone are of little value if the child cannot move around the environment with relative skill and ease. Children who can travel independently generally gain in self-confidence, physical development, social growth, and school achievement over children who must constantly depend on others to "get around."

There are four basic ways in which a person with a visual loss can travel:

1. Some visually impaired persons travel completely *on their own.* Blind children can usually learn to travel independently around familiar places, such as the home and school, relying on touch and their sense of direction. We can help children develop good independent travel skills.

Partially sighted children can learn to use their residual vision for traveling around. Some may benefit from mobility instruction, particularly for crossing streets, traveling in crowded places, and encountering other potentially dangerous situations.

2. Most visually impaired children need to depend on a sighted person as a *guide* at certain times. You can demonstrate, for your class, the proper way to walk with a visually impaired person:

Hold your arms downward in a relaxed position. The visually impaired person will place his/her hand lightly on your arm, at or near your elbow, and will walk slightly behind and to one side of you. You don't need to change your natural walking style at all! It isn't necessary to say to the visually impaired person, "We're coming to a hill," "We're turning left," or "We're stepping down the curb." He/she will feel these changes and react accordingly.

Never push or pull a visually impaired child.

3. The long cane is a widely used and effective device for assisting the visually impaired person in independent travel. The person "sweeps" the cane back and forth while walking, lightly touching it to the ground ahead.

In this way, visually impaired persons can travel in a straight direction detecting such features as curbs, buildings, paths, walls, and obstacles. Painted white, the cane also alerts drivers to the traveler for added safety.

There are many skills and techniques in cane travel. . .

. . .and instruction should be given by a qualified orientation and mobility specialist. In general, the earlier a
visually impaired child can receive such instruction, the
better. Eleven or twelve years of age is a good starting
time for mobility instruction.

4. About 10% of visually impaired persons travel with the aid of *guide dogs.* They are generally not available to children under sixteen.

Stick with me baby, and I'll show you the town.

These dogs are bred and trained at special agencies. The person and dog must take part in an intensive training period together which lasts for several weeks. To effectively use a guide dog, a visually impaired person should be in good physical condition, have a good sense of direction, be able to give verbal instructions to the dog, and care for the dog suitably.

Not every visually impaired person can or should have a guide dog. The dog is most valuable in situations where the user frequently travels through unfamiliar and complicated areas, as in large cities. Few visually impaired students in local schools are likely to have guide dogs.

Some visually impaired children like to clap their hands, click their tongues, or snap their fingers while walking in the halls in school. This may seem funny or strange to you. Actually, such sharp sounds can help the child travel - by hearing the way in which the sounds echo, the child can tell how far away the walls are and gain other clues about the surrounding area. This built-in "sonar system" can help alert the child to obstacles.

Many visually impaired people learn to use their senses of hearing and touch to detect obstacles in their path. There is nothing mysterious or unusual about this - you would also rely on your remaining senses if you were deprived of vision.

Weather conditions can affect the visually impaired child's ability to travel. Snow and ice change the physical environment substantially. Snow, rain, and heavy winds also alter the sounds upon which a visually impaired child often depends.

In the classroom, you can help the visually impaired child locate something by giving verbal directions. Remember that the terms "left" and "right" should be in relationship to the child's body, not necessarily yours.

BRAILLE

Children who are totally blind, or who have too little vision to read print, learn to read and write using *braille.* Most blind children in local schools receive braille instruction through specialized teachers or agencies. Here are some things about braille that you, as a teacher in an integrated classroom, may find interesting and useful to know.

Braille is a system of touch reading which involves feeling raised dots. It was developed in 1829 by Louis Braille, a blind man. Other methods of touch reading for the blind have been tried before and since then, but braille is by far the most efficient, and is used all over the world. A blind person can read braille much faster than he/she could read by feeling raised or embossed letters.

ENGLISH BRAILLE CHARACTERS

1st LINE	a	b	c	d	e	f	g	h	i	j

2nd LINE	k	l	m	n	o	p	q	r	s	t

3rd LINE	u	v	x	y	z	and	for	of	the	with

4th LINE	ch	gh	sh	th	wh	ed	er	ou	ow	w

5th LINE:

,	;	:	.		!	( )	" ?	in	"
ea	be	con	dis	en		gg			
	bb	cc	dd		ff				

6th LINE:

Fraction-line sign		Numeral sign	Poetry sign	Apostrophe	Hyphen
st	ing	ble	ar		com

7th LINE:

Accent sign	Used in forming Contractions:			Italic or Decimal-point sign	Letter sign	Capital sign

In English braille, each letter of the alphabet has a different symbol made with dots. In addition, there are many other braille symbols and abbreviations called contractions.

" W Y Be MY FR "

MEANS

" WILL YOU BE MY FRIEND ? "

Contractions, like shorthand, help save time and space. Frequently used words, such as *and, the, for, in,* and *with;* and combinations of letters such as *sh, th, ed, er, ow, ing,* and *tion,* have their own distinct symbols. Today, children are generally taught these symbols and contractions as soon as they begin to learn braille.

Braille has many rules of usage. The same dots may have several different meanings, depending on how they are used. For example ⠒⠒ may mean *cc, con,* or : (colon). ⠵ may mean *z* or *as*.

There are special forms of braille that can be used for music, mathematics, science, and foreign languages.

Braille dots can be punched using a slate and stylus.

However, it is preferable to use a *brailler,* a machine that looks something like a typewriter with six keys - one for each dot in the braille cell.

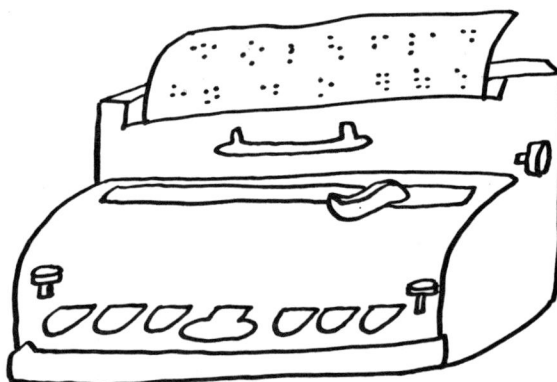

A student who uses braille regularly should have his/her own brailler. They are usually loaned free of charge through state or local agencies serving the visually impaired. Braillers can also be purchased from:

Howe Press of Perkins School for the Blind
175 North Beacon Street
Watertown, Massachusetts 02172

Braillers cost about the same as a good portable typewriter.

SPECIAL CONSIDERATIONS FOR
THE PARTIALLY SIGHTED

Let's now consider some of the special problems of the partially sighted child - the child who has a significant visual loss, but enough sight to learn to read print.

Partially sighted children's needs are different from those of blind children and children with normal vision. Since they fall between these two groups, partially sighted children are often misunderstood. In some ways, partially sighted children may have greater educational and adjustment problems than totally blind children.

Some years ago, partially sighted children were often placed in "sight saving" classes. The idea was:

Since you only have a little bit of sight we must save it. Be careful ... don't use your eyes too much! REMEMBER, boys and girls — if you use it, you could lose it !!

Sometimes, partially sighted children were even blind-folded or placed in dark rooms, and forced to learn braille, as if they were totally blind.

Today we know that the old "sight saving" approach was largely unwise. Partially sighted children should not be treated as though they are blind. *Vision does not decrease with use;* in fact, the opposite is usually true. Eye specialists agree that the eyes, even if impaired, benefit from being used. The partially sighted child should be encouraged to *use* his/her vision in school unless otherwise directed by an optometrist or ophthalmologist.

Here are some suggestions for the partially sighted child in your classroom:

• The child's desk or working area should be well lighted. Except for a few eye conditions which make children sensitive to bright lights, the partially sighted child usually benefits from plentiful, evenly distributed, glare-free illumination.

•Desks with adjustable tops are almost essential, since constant bending over a flat desk can result in fatigue and discomfort. The desk top should be close enough and comfortable so that it reduces glare and shadow. An alternative is to place an easel atop the desk for reading and writing.

- Special writing paper is available for the partially sighted. It should be of a dull finish with widely-spaced green lines.

- Felt or nylon-tipped markers, black ball point pens, and thick pencils with soft lead are helpful for written work. Let the child try several different kinds of writing instruments and papers. The visually impaired child will usually find one he/she prefers.

• Reading and writing at a desk are tiring for many partially sighted children. It is advisable for some children to do part of their written work at the chalkboard if they can see the work more clearly. They may find this a relaxing change. Use thick, soft, white chalk on a green chalkboard, if possible.

• Most partially sighted children benefit from learning manuscript writing first. This helps them differentiate between letters and words that look similar. Cursive writing can be taught later.

- Typewriters with large, clear type are helpful for the child and teacher in preparing written assignments.

- Partially sighted children may have difficulty keeping their place in a book.

Some children can read more easily with a bookmark placed just above the line that is being read. Others can read through a slot in a piece of dark paper which exposes a line or two of print at a time.

• Don't worry about the child getting "too close" to the paper. He/she will find the reading and writing position that is most comfortable.

Some children need to get very close to the material.

Some may squint. Others with poor central vision read best out of the corner of the eye. This may appear awkward, but it is probably the best position possible for them.

• Many large print books are available from publishers, libraries, and the American Printing House for the Blind. Various print sizes are used. It is recommended that the child not use print that is any larger than necessary, since with very large print only a small amount or "span" of reading can be taken in at a time. The child should ordinarily use the smallest print size that he/she can comfortably read. Many partially sighted students, in fact, prefer standard print.

•Many partially sighted children, though not all, can benefit from special "low vision aids" in the classroom. These may include special glasses, contact lenses, magnifiers, binoculars, telescopes, and other devices. *There is no one aid that is "right" for all children.* Some children are not helped by such aids and should not be compelled to use them. Clinics specializing in low vision can determine which type of aid, if any, is appropriate for the child. Low vision aids should be used only when essential.

Most schools have overhead projectors that use transparencies. The child with limited vision may find it helpful to look directly into the projector (from behind it), while the transparency is projected on the wall for the rest of the class.

Recently developed devices which can also aid the partially sighted include closed circuit television magnifiers, rear-view projection screens, and microfilm viewers. These are expensive, however, and not generally available in schools with a small number of visually impaired students.

A useful address to know is: American Printing House for the Blind, 1839 Frankfort Avenue, Louisville, KY 40206.

You can obtain a catalog of the many books, magazines . . .

. . .tape recordings, and other materials available for blind and partially sighted students simply by writing to the American Printing House for the Blind.

"Talking Book Machines" are record players adapted especially for use by blind and other physically handicapped persons. Many educational and recreational books are available. The machines and records are loaned free of charge through your state or regional Library for the Blind and Physically Handicapped.

• Reading readiness activities for visually impaired children are much like those for sighted children; these begin at the kindergarten level or sooner. In the early elementary grades much reading is done aloud, so the child is at less of a disadvantage than later in school, when most reading is done silently. Encourage reading. . .the visually impaired child will benefit from frequent practice of reading skills.

Teachers often ask, "How fast can a child read braille?" There is no exact answer. Reading rate depends on the child and the level of difficulty of the material. Studies of braille readers in elementary and junior high schools often show an average reading rate of about 100 words per minute, but this can vary from below 40 to above 200 words per minute.

In most cases it is not absolutely necessary for the regular classroom teacher to learn braille. The visually impaired student may use a typewriter for written assignments, or your program may have an itinerant or resource teacher who knows braille. It is certainly helpful, however, if the regular teacher can read braille. If you are interested in learning, you might ask the special teacher - or perhaps even your visually impaired student - to teach you. Most people find that braille is not as difficult to learn as it seems at first. The sighted person can read braille by looking at the raised dots rather than by feeling them.

BRAILLE   LARGE PRINT

SEE THE CAT.

Teachers and parents sometimes ask whether a child who is losing his/her vision gradually - and may later become totally blind - should be taught braille. This is a very difficult question, educationally and emotionally. First of all, medical consultation with ophthalmologists should be promptly sought to make sure the eye condition is correctly diagnosed, and to save vision through medical or surgical treatment if at all possible. We recommend that such a child continue to learn in all areas - including reading, writing, and travel - by using his/her vision for as long as possible. The skills and concepts the child learns will serve him/her well if blindness does occur at some future time. In general we have not found it advisable to teach braille while the student still has enough vision to read print.

New and exciting devices - such as the "reading machine," "talking" math calculator, compressed speech, and of course, radios, tapes, and cassettes - make it possible for the visually impaired person to receive a large amount of information through listening. Will modern technology eventually replace braille completely? Probably not. While such devices can greatly enrich the person's education and experience, it is still important for him/her to have the active, personal involvement with reading and writing that braille offers.

ARRANGING YOUR CLASSROOM

In the integrated classroom, you will not have to make major changes in the physical environment for the visually impaired child. A few suggestions, however, are offered for safety and practical reasons:

• Show the new visually impaired child around the room, pointing out where different features are located. Let the child become oriented to the surroundings.

... and back here is the pool table and bar...

- Try to keep the area free of dangerous obstacles.

- Half-open doors are hazardous for the visually impaired. Keep them fully open or closed.

- Don't enter or leave the room without telling the visually impaired child.

- The visually impaired child will help you keep things where they belong! It's good practice to have an orderly classroom, but you don't need to be rigid about the environment. Change things around from time to time, tell the child, and let him/her become familiar with the new arrangements.

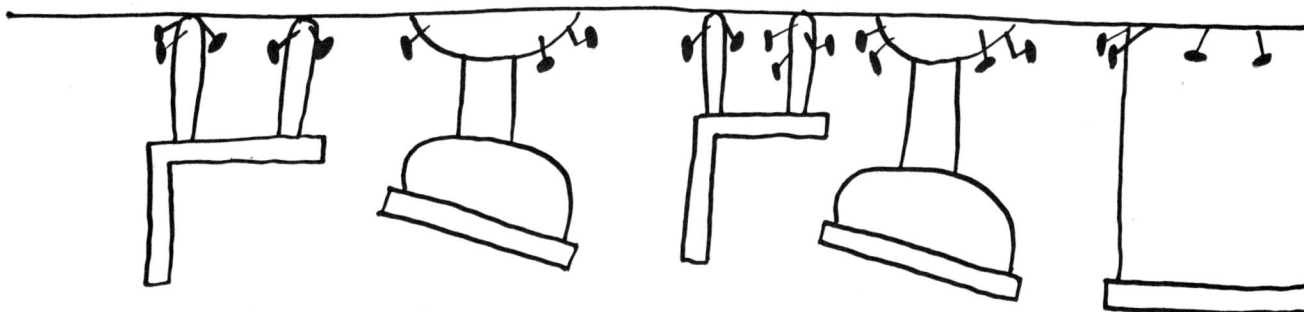

We've made a few minor arrangements, but it shouldn't take you long to get familiar with them.

- It's fun to have a table or area with interesting, changing displays and materials for the children to explore and manipulate on their own.

- If you assign daily responsibilities to your students, make sure to include the visually impaired child. The child can take a turn emptying the wastebaskets, feeding the gerbils, cleaning the erasers, watering the plants, and so on.

• Take a little extra time to familiarize your new visually
impaired student with the fire drill procedures in your
school. It may be helpful for him/her to pair up with a
buddy and practice leaving the room quickly. Loud
bells or sirens can startle and frighten some visually
impaired children, especially if they don't know what
the sound means.

•It's important for a visually impaired child to have a place to call his/her own. Provide a desk, locker, or cubbyhole where the child may keep things. Let him/her explore the area. Respect privacy as you would that of any other child. A locker at the very end of a row is easy to locate.

SOUND PROOF

• If possible, it may be a good idea to set aside a small adjoining room or partitioned area for times when the visually impaired student does independent class work, or receives individual help from a special teacher or classmate. During quiet periods, the noise of a brailler or someone reading aloud may be distracting to other students. Conversely, the visually impaired child may find it difficult to concentrate if there is excessive background noise. Be careful, though, not to isolate the visually impaired student from classmates too much of the time, since this would defeat many of the positive aspects of mainstreaming.

● You may wonder why visually impaired children do not have accidents. If you were suddenly blindfolded, you would be likely to have accidents. . .

YE-E-O-OW!!

. . .but the blind or partially sighted child has gradually learned to negotiate the environment, taking into consideration his/her degree of visual loss, and can usually avoid serious accidents and injuries.

Nobody enjoys seeing a visually impaired child fall or get bumped or bruised - but this happens to all children. It would be far worse to overprotect the child and restrict his/her movement, depriving the child of freedom, curiosity, and a wide variety of experiences.

APPROACHES TO TEACHING

The visually impaired child may miss out on many concepts and sources of information. If the child hears a dog bark, for example, but cannot see it, he/she may not know whether the dog is large or small, leashed or unleashed, angry or friendly.

Visually impaired children who do not have certain things explained or interpreted for them not only suffer educationally, but may tend to lose confidence and become withdrawn, passive, or overly dependent in their behavior.

Often it is necessary to deliberately plan "connecting events" for the visually impaired. For example, a child who has often eaten cooked carrots. . .

. . .and raw carrots. . .

. . .may not be aware that these rather different tastes come from the same vegetable. . .

. . .or may not know that carrots are grown by planting seeds in the ground. Lessons and projects which can demonstrate such concepts are extremely useful to the visually impaired child, as they help "fill the gaps" in his/her understanding.

A child with little or no vision is not able to learn through observation and imitation in the same way as a child with good vision.

Field trips are also of much value to the visually impaired student at all grade levels. Whether it's a trip to the fire station, dairy, bakery, bank, hospital, airport, radio station, museum, or state capitol, such outings greatly enhance the student's knowledge of the community, the world, and the various jobs people do.

You may be surprised at how much your visually impaired child gains from field trips, even to places you may think of as largely visual.

If you plan field trips in advance, you will find that most places are pleased to have visually impaired students among their visitors. Your hosts may even provide some extra things to hear, touch, smell, or taste which can make the visit more meaningful for all your students.

Successful teachers of visually impaired children in local schools constantly use imagination and communication for the benefit of all their students. The visually impaired child is in a position to make good use of your help. He/she is not "cut off" from the many experiences and interactions that occur in your classroom every day. The child may even help you become a better teacher!

Most of us gain information and form impressions about other people by looking at their faces. We can often tell whether someone is cheerful, tense, interested, sad, worried, or bored by looking at his or her facial expression. The child with little or no vision, however, gains his/her most meaningful impressions about people from their tone of voice. He/she may quickly sense the emotion in your voice, and react to it. Sighted people sometimes suppose that the blind are very interested in touching other people's faces. This is not usually true.

With some visually impaired children - particularly those
who were born blind - their facial expression may not
accurately indicate what they are feeling or thinking. The
way in which they hold their hands and fingers may give
you better clues to their emotional state.

- If you are speaking to the visually impaired child in a group, be sure to address him/her by name. Otherwise, the child may not realize for whom your remarks are intended.

Can you tell me the first person singular of...

I sure hope he calls on me. I know that one.

• If the visually impaired child cannot see the chalkboard, it's easy and helpful to say the words or describe the figures aloud as you write. This helps the child follow along with the rest of the class.

The teacher is in a good position to notice the day-to-day visual functioning of all students, and should be aware if changes occur in the handicapped child's vision. *If the child complains of eye pain, or does not seem to be seeing as well as he/she did previously, it's important to arrange for a thorough eye examination promptly. Certain conditions, such as glaucoma, can lead to a total loss of vision if not detected and treated medically.*

Some visually impaired children wear prostheses ("artificial eyes") if one or both eyes have been removed. Ordinarily, the child is able to care for them easily. If the eyes are often runny, swollen, or inflamed, it could indicate that the prosthesis is no longer fitting well, and a reexamination by the prosthetist should be suggested.

Many kinds of tests are used in schools. They can be *misused,* too. Some tests are unfair or inappropriate for the child with little or no sight. Intelligence tests, in particular, often rely heavily on visual concepts. They may not give an accurate picture of a visually impaired child's true abilities. They may need to be modified.

Always use caution in giving tests and in interpreting a child's previous test results. Unfortunately, many visually impaired children have been the victims of unwise educational placement decisions because of their performance on tests.

chapter 3

---

areas
of
curriculum

Certain adaptations or modifications are advisable in teaching various subjects to the visually impaired. It's impossible here, of course, to deal with all curricular areas at all age and grade levels. Instead we will present a few general suggestions for your consideration. Where specific difficulties arise, a specialist in the education of the visually impaired may be able to help you with instructional materials and resources.

READING

In reading activities, always emphasize *thinking.* Interject appropriate questions such as, "What do you know about this subject?", or "How do you suppose the story will end?" Such communication helps the child relate his/her own experiences to the material and helps you monitor comprehension.

Avoid using one medium constantly, as this can be tiring. Vary reading activities by using braille or print, reading aloud, group participation, and records or tapes. Always encourage expressiveness in reading rather than "word-calling."

Allow adequate time for the visually impaired child to complete reading assignments.

MATH

Many "new math" approaches are quite appropriate for the visually impaired child, as they emphasize reasoning skills and the use of concrete materials rather than pencil-and-paper calculations. The solving of practical problems is always important.

Visually impaired students often use the abacus for arithmetic computation.

It is important for visually impaired students to know the denominations of coins and paper money and to be able to use them in everyday situations. Practice transactions which involve the giving and receiving of change.

ANTE UP !!

In general, accuracy is more important than speed for the visually impaired math student. Tests or assignments should present a reasonable number of varied problems rather than repetitive problems of the same kind.

SOCIAL STUDIES

Social studies presentations can greatly enrich the child's awareness of the world.

Community persons or museum staff members may be able to visit your class and bring interesting things to discuss and touch.

Lessons about the customs, music, dances, costumes, and food of people in other countries, or from earlier periods in history, are enjoyable and lend themselves well to participation.

Raised drawings, diagrams, and maps are often useful. Sometimes though, they can give misleading impressions. They should be used parallel to the floor, as on a table, rather than hanging on a wall.

YO-DA-LA-EE-HOO

RELIEF MAP

Allow visually impaired children to explore pictures and items tactually on their own. Don't "help" them by pushing, pulling, or rushing their hands over the material.

The older visually impaired student will find it most valuable to take part in real or simulated activities which help him/her to understand such things as:

- Obtaining a social security card
- Filling out employment applications
- Going for a job interview
- Completing income tax forms
- Maintaining a bank account
- Registering to vote
- Comparison shopping for good values

If your class subscribes to educational periodicals such as *My Weekly Reader, You and Your World,* or *Senior Scholastic,* you may be interested to know that these and many other publications are available in braille and large print editions.

SCIENCE

Science activities are often tactual in nature, and lend themselves well to participation by the visually impaired. It's a good idea for the visually impaired child to have a sighted partner in laboratory experiments.

Plants and pets are useful and fun. The child can notice changes in the size, texture, or odor of the plant, animal, or soil. Experiments or projects involving concepts of nutrition, reproduction, and ecology can be devised.

• Trips to museums, weather stations, planetariums, and other places are valuable for information that may be experienced or explained.

... and that's a weather balloon.

- Scales, pulleys, relief maps, globes, models of the human body and solar system, and many other appropriate materials are available or may be constructed in school.

- Visually impaired children are often interested in weather conditions. Have them keep daily records of the temperature, humidity, and rainfall.

MUSIC

Some - though by no means all - visually impaired children are talented and interested in music. They can gain from, and contribute to, such group activities as the chorus, band, or orchestra, and social, folk, or square dancing.

PHYSICAL EDUCATION AND RECREATION

Physical Education and Recreation are extremely important to the child with a visual impairment. Experience in motor skills greatly assists the student in his/her mobility and self-confidence. Visually impaired persons can participate in most athletic and recreational activities enjoyed by the sighted. Good posture and muscle tone should be encouraged.

• Wrestling and track are sports in which the visually impaired can readily compete against sighted athletes. A blind runner may be guided by lightly feeling a rope or railing along the edge of the track.

• Visually impaired students often enjoy roller skating and ice skating. Music can aid their orientation if speakers are placed at different locations around the gym or skating rink.

•Tandem bicycles are fun and good exercise. The visually impaired child rides in the rear, while a sighted friend takes the front seat.

• Audible balls are available. By listening to a bell or signal inside the ball, the visually impaired child may be able to play quite a good game of catch, or even a modified form of basefall.

WHAT'S HAPPENIN' BABY?

• Some students become proficient at basketball by listening to a metronome or other constantly ticking device placed at or near the basket.

• Blind and partially sighted children find the trampoline enjoyable and valuable. Station sighted observers at each edge. The children can locate the center of the trampoline more easily if a small bell is attached to the underside of it.

•Swimming should be available to every visually impaired child. A child with little or no sight generally enjoys much more freedom of movement in the water than on land. Normal safety precautions – usually involving a buddy system – should be followed.

• There are many successful blind bowlers, golfers, and skiers! Usually a sighted companion provides certain assistance, as in locating or describing the situation.

Playing cards, Scrabble, Monopoly, and many other popular educational and recreational games are available in braille or can be easily adapted for use by the visually impaired.

LISTENING SKILLS

Listening Skills are very important. They can make the difference between a child being "included in" and "left out of" an activity. A visually impaired child sitting in a regular classroom will not automatically develop effective listening skills. Sometimes these skills may have to be deliberately developed and practiced.

Many visually impaired children are fond of listening to the radio at home and at school. They often obtain useful information this way. However, the radio should *not* be used constantly to "kill time." The child also needs to hear things going on in the environment, and to become involved with people. Continuous radio listening tends to discourage children's curiosity and exploration.

GROWING UP

Visually impaired students at all grade levels need realistic knowledge about the world of work and possible areas of employment. Today successful visually impaired persons may be found in almost all professions and occupations. A young totally blind man was recently graduated from medical school. Teachers and counselors should not suggest stereotyped, limited employment roles. It is always helpful for students to have direct contact with people from various career fields.

If your school offers educational programs in sex education, alcohol and drug abuse, and related areas, the visually impaired student should participate to the same extent as other students. Such programs are often largely visual in nature, and may presume a degree of prior knowledge that the visually impaired student does not possess. Supplemental instruction and counseling can be helpful.

In working with the visually impaired, it's always wise to keep in mind the importance of basic skills. Will our student be able to go to the supermarket, buy food, and prepare a meal?

Can he/she make good use of leisure time?

Is the visually impaired student able to make independent decisions and assume responsibilities?

Does the student project a favorable image to other people through his/her personal appearance and behavior?

If we must answer "no" to these questions, we may be neglecting some very critical aspects of our student's education.

In
Closing . . .

Teachers can best assist parents of their visually impaired students by keeping the "channels of communication" between home and school open and positive. An occasional note or phone call to let the parents know that Beth is doing well with her fractions, or that Ron just got a good role in the school play can facilitate communication when problems do arise. Most parents are anxious to see their children succeed in school, and can help you in many ways. Encourage parents to visit your class. Avoid making constant or unrealistic demands on parents, however - they may have many responsibilities in addition to those of caring for their visually impaired child. Be a good listener. Concerned parents can tell you much about their child's functioning. They are not telling you how to teach, but rather how their child learns.

Ask yourself from time to time, "What is the *real* comprehension level of this student?" Handicapped students in local schools have sometimes been promoted from grade to grade for social reasons - so that they can be with their friends - rather than for sound academic reasons. We do our students a disservice if we overlook their problem areas, lower our standards, or do their work for them. This does not help them acquire the skills and knowledge they will need.

A wide variety of educational, vocational, financial, and related services are available to visually impaired children, their families, and their teachers. If you are not familiar with the resources in your area, contact your state's Department of Special Education or Commission for the Visually Handicapped. We strongly encourage you – and your visually impaired students – to take advantage of the services and benefits available.

"Mainstreaming" the visually impaired student, as we have learned, is a real challenge. There is no single approach that is "right" for all situations. It often seems difficult to meet each child's unique needs, encourage interaction, and maintain a well-balanced educational program for all students at the same time. Mainstreaming may not even be the best educational alternative for some visually impaired students—particularly those with multiple disabilities. Yet we believe it deserves to be tried. We believe that the integrated classroom is an environment that can help make living and learning richer for the visually impaired child, as well as for his/her sighted friends.

Our best wishes go to you, the teacher, who, with understanding, imagination, and hard work can accept this challenge and make mainstreaming a reality.

BIBLIOGRAPHY

Bishop, V. E. *Teaching the visually limited child.* Springfield, Illinois: Charles C Thomas, 1971.

Cholden, L. S. *A psychiatrist works with blindness.* New York: American Foundation for the Blind, 1958.

Cohoe, E. Newer methods of teaching reading to the partially seeing child. *Exceptional Children,* 1960, *1,* 11-17.

Deitz, S. J. *Handbook for volunteers.* Medford, Oregon: Jackson County Intermediate Education District, 1974.

DeMott, R. M. Visually impaired. In N. G. Haring (Ed.) *Behavior of exceptional children.* Columbus, Ohio: Charles E. Merrill, 1974.

Dinnage, R. *The handicapped child: Research review volume II.* London: Longman Group Limited, 1972.

Hanninen, K. A. *Teaching the visually handicapped.* Columbus, Ohio: Charles E. Merrill, 1975.

Harley, R. K., Jr. Children with visual disabilities. In L. M. Dunn (Ed.) *Exceptional children in the schools: Special education in transition.* New York: Holt, Rinehart and Winston, 1974.

Hatlen, P. H. Priorities in education programs for visually handicapped children and youth. *Division for the Visually Handicapped Newsletter* (Council for Exceptional Children), Winter, 1976, *20*(3), 8-11.

Hewett, F. M., with Forness, S. R. *Education of exceptional learners.* Boston: Allyn and Bacon, 1974.

Lansdown, R. What the research doesn't know. *Special Education* (London), 1969, *4,* 20-24.

Lowenfeld, B. *Our blind children.* Springfield, Illinois: Charles C Thomas, 1964.

McDonald, S. & Parnell, D. *The blind student in the regular classroom: A guide for teachers and students.* Victoria, B. C.: Government of British Columbia, Department of Education, 1976.

Moor, P. M. *A blind child, too, can go to nursery school.* New York: American Foundation for the Blind, 1952.

Napier, G. D. Special subject adjustments and skills. In B. Lowenfeld (Ed) *The visually handicapped child in school.* New York: John Day, 1973.

Scott, E. *The partially sighted student in school: A guide for teachers.* Toronto: Canadian National Institute for the Blind, 1976.

Seamons, G. R. *Swimming for the blind.* Provo, Utah: Bringham Young University, 1966.

About the Editor

Thomas N. Fairchild, has his Ph.D. in School Psychology and is currently an Assistant Professor of Counseling and Guidance and Coordinator of the School of Psychology Training Program at the University of Idaho. Dr. Fairchild earned his Bachelors, Masters, and Specialist degrees at the University of Idaho. He received his Ph.D. from the University of Iowa in 1974. The editor has published over a dozen journal articles in the areas of school psychology and counseling. Dr. Fairchild has worked as a teacher, counselor, and school psychologist. He has had the privilege of working with students across all grade levels, and in his opinion they are all special.

About the Author

Michael D. Orlansky received his Bachelor's degree from Yale University, his Master's degree from Boston College, and his Ph.D. with emphasis in special education from the University of Idaho. His interest in visually impaired children began in 1966, when he was a counselor at Camp Wapanaki, a summer program for blind children in Vermont. He taught for four years at the Perkins School for the Blind in Watertown, Massachusetts, and later served as a teacher and educational specialist for deaf-blind children in the state of Washington. He has participated extensively in workshops and inservice training programs for teachers of visually impaired children. In the U.S. Air Force, Mike taught English as a Second Language to foreign students. Mike is currently an Assistant Professor in the Department of Special Education at the University of Virginia and resides in Charlottesville, Virginia, with his wife, Janice, and daughter, Tamar.

About the Illustrator

Everyone can draw—some with more competence than others. Occasionally you find someone who is exceptionally gifted in a particular facet of drawing. Danial B. Fairchild is that someone. He is a highly talented cartoonist with a style that is uniquely his own. Among his achievements include cartoons printed in newspapers and magazines, and most recently two paperbacks entitled **Cowtoons** (Artcraft Press, Nampa, Idaho), which depict in a very humorous way the life of cowboys.

121